SPOTLIGHT ON NATIVE AMERICANS

NAVAJO

Amarie Kyle

PowerKiDS
press.

New York

Published in 2016 by The Rosen Publishing Group, Inc.
29 East 21st Street, New York, NY 10010

First Edition

Editor: Karolena Bielecki
Book Design: Kris Everson
Reviewed by: Robert J. Conley, Former Sequoyah Distinguished Professor at Western Carolina University and Director of Native American Studies at Morningside College and Montana State University
Supplemental material reviewed by: Donald A. Grinde, Jr., Professor of Transnational/American Studies at the State University of New York at Buffalo.

Photo Credits: Cover Jose Gil/Shutterstock.com; pp. 4–5 Julien Hautcoeur/Shutterstock.com; p. 7 (both) North Wind Picture Archives; p. 9 © Image Asset Management/World History Archive/age fotostock; p. 11 Peter Newark's American Pictures; p. 12 Native Stock; pp. 14, 17, 19, 21, 25, 26 Corbis; pp. 16–17 © Image Asset Management/World History Archive/age fotostock; pp. 22–23 jessicakirsh/Shutterstock.com; p. 29 Paul Thompson/Photolibrary/Getty Images.

Library of Congress Cataloging-in-Publication Data

Kyle, Amarie.
  Navajo / Amarie Kyle.
    pages cm. — (Spotlight on Native Americans)
  Includes bibliographical references and index.
  ISBN 978-1-4994-1691-6 (pbk.)
  ISBN 978-1-4994-1690-9 (6 pack)
  ISBN 978-1-4994-1693-0 (library binding)
  1. Navajo Indians—History—Juvenile literature. 2. Navajo Indians—Social life and customs—Juvenile literature. I. Title.
  E99.N3K95 2016
  979.1004'9726—dc23
                        2015008153

Manufactured in the United States of America

CPSIA Compliance Information: Batch #WS15PK: For Further Information contact Rosen Publishing, New York, New York at 1-800-237-9932

CONTENTS

NAVAJO ORIGINS

CHAPTER 1

The Navajos are a North American native people, most of whom now live on the Navajo **Reservation**, which covers large portions of northeastern Arizona, southeastern Utah, and northwestern New Mexico. Numbering more than 200,000, they are the largest reservation-based Indian nation in North America. Only the Cherokees have more tribal members, but they are not based on a reservation.

No one knows exactly how or when Navajos and other Native Americans came to the Americas, but like many ancient **cultures**, Navajos tell a story to explain their

origins. Navajos believe they have passed through three previous worlds to the present fourth one, which they call the Glittering World. In each of the previous worlds, a lack of harmony among the inhabitants caused them to leave. Living in harmony with the world—and with other Navajos—is an important part of Navajo culture.

"Navajo" is thought to be a word from the Zuni Pueblo Indian language, meaning "enemy." The Navajo word for themselves is "Diné," meaning "the people." In 1969, the Navajo Tribal Council officially adopted the name "Navajo Nation."

Monument Valley is a famous landmark in the desert country of the Southwest near the Navajo Reservation.

LIFE IN THE SOUTHWEST
CHAPTER 2

The Navajo have proven to be one of the most adaptable people in the world. Their adjustment to life in the desert Southwest is an example of that.

Before coming to the Southwest, the Navajos were hunter-gatherers. The men hunted, while the women gathered nuts, berries, wild onions, and other food. Upon their arrival in the Southwest, their culture was still similar to that of their close relatives, the Apaches.

Navajos apparently entered the Southwest at about the time of changes in the great Anasazi civilization of cliff dwellers. Partly because of a severe **drought** in the late 1300s, the Anasazis moved their farming communities to areas with more dependable water supplies near rivers and became known as the Pueblo people.

Those Pueblo people had a great impact on the Navajos, teaching them farming. Later, when the Spanish introduced sheep and the Pueblos learned to weave blankets and clothing, they passed those skills on to the Navajos.

From the Spanish, the Navajos acquired sheep, soon becoming expert shepherds with huge flocks. All of these

(Left) This woodcut shows Pueblo Indian farmers in New Mexico watching over their fields. The Pueblos remain among the most skillful dry farmers in the world. *(Right)* Navajos learned from the Pueblos that before wool can be woven into rugs on a **loom**, it must first be spun into wool thread.

new skills—farming, herding, and weaving—brought great changes to the Navajo way of life. By the 1700s, the Navajos were distinctly different from their Apache neighbors.

CONFLICTS WITH COLONIZERS

CHAPTER 3

By the late 1500s, the Spanish had conquered much of Mexico, but the Navajos, in today's northwestern New Mexico, were too far away from areas of Spanish exploration to be much affected by it. When the Spanish began settling in New Mexico in 1598, however, Navajos soon began to feel their impact.

Throughout the 1600s and 1700s, the Spanish made slave **raids** against the Navajos, stealing the women and children and killing the men. To meet this threat, the Navajos stole horses from the Spanish and became expert horsemen. By the late 1600s, the Navajos began raiding Spanish ranches, stealing their horses, sheep, and cattle. This made Spanish attacks against them more difficult.

The Spanish never conquered the Navajos. However, when the United States defeated Mexico in a war in 1848 and acquired New Mexico and Arizona as territories, Navajo life changed dramatically. Americans soon built forts in Navajo country, and settlers began

Edward S. Curtis took this photo of Navajos, calling it *Out of the Darkness*. Curtis was the most famous photographer of Native Americans of the late nineteenth and early twentieth centuries, taking thousands of pictures **documenting** native life.

pouring into the Southwest. The Navajos, who are a proud, freedom-loving people, soon found themselves in conflict with a great military power—one that was determined to force its will on native people.

DESTRUCTION OF LAND
CHAPTER 4

American soldiers seized land for their animals to graze on, pushing some Navajos off their land. When the Indians stood up for themselves, fighting broke out. To make matters worse, the United States was soon torn apart during the **American Civil War**. The value of any life seemed cheap amid the brutal battles of the war.

The U.S. Army decided to end Navajo resistance by destroying their homeland. In 1863, Colonel Kit Carson, who disagreed with the policy but carried it out anyway, led an army through the Navajo homeland. They burned houses, destroyed crops, killed livestock, and even chopped down fruit trees.

By 1864, several thousand Navajos had fled to remote areas farther west, while about 8,000 starving Navajos had surrendered to the U.S. Army. They were forced to walk about 300 miles (483 km) across New Mexico to the Bosque Redondo prison camp during the "Navajo Long Walk."

In 1868, the Navajos were finally allowed to **negotiate** their only treaty with the U.S. government. The treaty allowed them to return to their homeland, but by that time, many had died of disease in the prison camp. The surviving Navajos walked back to their destroyed homeland.

Shown here is an 1874 photo of Manuelito (1818–1894). A famous Navajo leader, he signed the Navajo treaty with the United States in 1868.

LIFE ON THE RESERVATION
CHAPTER 5

When the Navajos returned home to northwestern New Mexico from Bosque Redondo in 1868, the U.S. government provided them with sheep to begin

This photo shows Navajo students in the Carlisle Indian School Library. This boarding school was located in Pennsylvania, which is across the continent from the Navajo homeland.

rebuilding their flocks and with food to support them for 10 years. However, the treaty of 1868 reduced Navajo Nation land to 10 percent of what it once was. Over the next few decades, the United States increased the size of the reservation several times, but it remains much smaller than the old homeland.

One of the cruelest parts of reservation life was forcing Navajo children to attend boarding schools far from home. The boarding schools tried to turn Navajo children away from their culture—forcing them to learn the Christian religion and speak English. The children had to do all the labor at the schools—the cleaning, cooking, and farming that provided the food. In the 1930s, day schools on the reservation began replacing the boarding schools, and Navajo children were able to live at home while attending school.

Navajos had never had a centralized, national government. After oil was discovered on the reservation in 1921, however, the U.S. government forced them to form a government because it needed one to sign oil **leases**.

TRADITIONAL NAVAJO LIFESTYLE

CHAPTER 6

Navajo families are matriarchal, meaning that a woman, usually the grandmother, is the head of the household. When a son marries, he goes to live with his wife's family.

This photo, taken sometime during the first half of the twentieth century, shows women weaving blankets from wool on outdoor looms near their home. The outdoors were cooler and brighter than their hogan.

Navajo girls grow up learning that they will one day lead their family.

Made of wood, the typical traditional Navajo house is called a hogan. A hole in the center of the roof allows smoke to escape from the cooking fire. The doorway always faces the rising sun in the east. Navajos typically build a hogan in a valley for their winter home and another one near mountain **pastures**, which they live in during the summer months.

During the nineteenth century, Navajos developed distinctive styles of clothing. Women favored colorful blouses and skirts, while men wore jeans, boots, and colorful shirts. A black hat became very popular for men. Both men and women wore silver and turquoise jewelry, which is a distinctive Navajo tradition that is still very popular.

Navajos cook and sleep outside during the summers since the homeland is mostly desert. Women set up their weaving looms outdoors, under a pole structure, with a roof made of brush to provide shade.

CEREMONIES AND SONGS
CHAPTER 7

According to Navajo tradition, being out of harmony causes illness. Navajos consult experts, who are called hand tremblers or crystal gazers, can tell the nature of an illness and recommend the right healing ceremony to restore the patient to harmony. A medicine man, who is called a singer, will then conduct the ceremony.

As an example, one of the most famous ceremonies is the Enemy Way Ceremony for Navajo soldiers returning from war. The ceremony cleanses the soldier of the **contamination** of death and other evils from fighting.

Navajo healing ceremonies last several days and require many people as helpers, singers, and dancers. The principal

Navajo sand painting

singers must study for many years to memorize the songs and sand paintings for just one ceremony.

There are only a small number of singers to perform the different ceremonies. Few medicine men are able to learn more than one or two. Some ceremonies have been lost when the only singer who still knew them died.

The sand paintings are made on the ground with different colors of sand inside the family hogan. The person being healed sits in the middle of the sand painting, and the illness is transferred to the painting, which is then destroyed.

Making sand paintings requires years of study to learn the many different patterns used in just one ceremony.

IMPORTANCE OF THE CLAN
CHAPTER 8

Other ceremonies celebrate changes in life, such as a girl's **puberty** ceremony, which is called a *kinaalda*. All of the girl's relatives participate in the celebration of her entry into womanhood, which is one of the most important events in her life. The *kinaalda* features songs and dances, and it lasts for several days.

Ceremonies are very expensive because the family hosting one must feed many people for up to nine days. They must also pay the principal singer a large fee, which is often paid in livestock. Holding a ceremony for someone is a serious decision, requiring the help and support of many relatives. Because so many family members and community members are involved, Navajo ceremonies also help create positive connections between people in the community.

Children get their clan membership from their parents. These clans spread out across the Navajo Nation, giving people extended family across the land. Clan membership carries responsibilities to and for

This woman is participating in the Spring Snow Ceremony in the mid-1960s. She is in the Luckachukai Mountains on the Navajo Reservation, which is along the border between Arizona and New Mexico.

other clan members. Since their traditional culture had no government, clan relationships were—and remain— very important.

NAVAJO LITERATURE AND ART

CHAPTER 9

Through literature and art, Navajos may very well have done more than any other tribe in expressing what it means to see the world through the eyes of their culture. Navajo author and storyteller Vee Browne has won awards for her children's versions of traditional Navajo stories. Beautifully illustrated, the books tell of the adventures of Navajo cultural heroes with names such as Monster Slayer and Born of Water.

The songs of the healing ceremonies are works of beautiful poetry. Handed down through **generations**, no one knows the names of the people who produced them. These songs were composed before Navajos had a written version of their language. The only way to learn them was to memorize them by studying with a singer as they chanted the songs. The first **poet laureate** of the Navajo Nation, Luci Tapahonso, was named in 2013.

This painting by Nelson Tsosie is titled *Silver Horizons*. Tsosie uses images from Navajo life in both his paintings and sculptures.

Another famous Navajo writer is Irvin Morris. His book, *From the Glittering World*, is used in college courses to learn about the Navajo view of the world.

The Navajo Nation has also produced famous Indian painters, including R. C. Gorman, Carl Nelson Gorman, and Paul Apodaca. The Navajo homeland is a strikingly beautiful place that comes alive in their work.

THE NAVAJO NATION

CHAPTER 10

When a formal government for the Navajo people was being created in the 1920s, one problem that had to be overcome was the great distances that separated Navajos from one another. Navajos were a rural people of widely scattered shepherding families. The plan that was adopted created more than 100 local units called Chapter Houses. Today, the Chapter Houses are still the basic foundation for the Navajo Nation government.

The Navajo Nation Council is the national legislature of the Navajo people, who also elect a president to

The famous window rock is located near the Navajo Nation capital at Window Rock, Arizona.

lead. The capital of the Navajo Nation is at Window Rock, in northeastern Arizona. The town is named for a famous rock formation that has a big hole in it like a window.

The Navajo Nation Tribal Police helps maintain law and order, and the Navajos have their own court system. The most serious crimes, however, are still investigated by the U.S. Federal Bureau of Investigation (FBI).

The nation also publishes its own newspaper, *The Navajo Times*. Several radio stations broadcast in the Navajo language, which is spoken by more than 200,000 people. With so many speakers, it is in no danger of being lost like so many other Indian languages.

THE NAVAJO RESERVATION TODAY

CHAPTER 11

The Navajo Reservation lies in a high-altitude desert dotted with mountains atop the Colorado Plateau. With cold winters and hot summers, it's a rugged, dry country.

The introduction of automobiles during the early twentieth century ended much of the isolation on the Navajo Reservation. However, only the main highways through the reservation are paved. Most of the reservation is still lonely backcountry, where horses can get to places cars cannot go.

Much of the reservation still does not have things that most Americans take for granted, such as electricity. People often still use fires to prepare food, and many still depend on their livestock to provide much of that food. Navajo children frequently take long bus rides to school.

With around half the population living in poverty, the Navajo Reservation has high suicide and alcoholism rates. Other problems are **diabetes**, which is four times more common on the reservation than in the United States in general, and cancers caused by **uranium** waste from mining.

This Navajo woman is demonstrating how to make fry bread over an open fire. Many Navajo women prefer outdoor cooking to indoor cooking.

The Navajos run their own health centers, which are now built to include rooms for traditional healers. In Shiprock, New Mexico, the Northern Navajo Medical Center treats hundreds of patients every day.

EDUCATION AND ECONOMY

CHAPTER 12

Many of the 150 public schools on the reservation are poor, and high numbers of students drop out of high school. However, the Navajo Preparatory School, Inc., in Farmington, New Mexico, is controlled by the Navajo Nation, and it takes only talented students

Shown here are children in a classroom at an elementary school on the reservation. Children are taught in Navajo as well as in English.

who intend to go on to colleges and universities. As well as demanding high academic standards from its students, the school offers courses in Navajo culture.

The federal and tribal governments are now the biggest employers on the Navajo Reservation, but stock raising and farming still provide many jobs. The tribe also operates an electronics business and a sawmill.

Tourism is not big business, although the Navajos own some campgrounds and sell fishing and hunting permits. There are many art and craft shops, and most Navajo families include people who make extra money from traditional skills, such as weaving and making silver jewelry.

Money from mining companies that pay to use Navajo land is a large portion of the Navajo Nation's income. In 2004, the Diné Development Corporation was formed to promote and help create Navajo businesses.

LOOKING TO THE FUTURE
CHAPTER 13

The Navajos and Hopis have long fought over the borders of the land in northeastern Arizona, which the two tribes once shared. Some Navajo families have been ordered to leave what is now Hopi land. In 2014, severe drought ignited the issue again when Navajo grazing animals were locked up after being caught on Hopi land.

The Navajo Nation has started a number of programs to provide jobs. One is a huge agricultural **irrigation** project in the San Juan River Valley in New Mexico to turn desert into cropland.

After many years, the Navajo Nation decided that the income and jobs casinos provide outweigh the disadvantages. The first casino opened in 2008. Today, there are several casinos in operation, all managed by the Navajo Nation Gaming Enterprise, which is a business organization owned by the nation.

Navajos are fortunate to still live in their **ancestral** homeland, unlike many other Indian tribes who were removed to Indian Territory (now Oklahoma). This has helped them maintain their culture. They persevere with confidence and pride—and with more control of their own destiny than many previous generations.

This photo shows a young Navajo girl in traditional clothing looking out across Monument Valley, Utah.

29

GLOSSARY

American Civil War: The war between northern and southern U.S. states that lasted from 1861 to 1865.

ancestral: Belonging to someone in your family who lived long before you.

contamination: The act of making something impure through contact with something bad.

culture: The arts, beliefs, and customs that form a people's way of life.

diabetes: A disease that causes problems with the body's ability to control the levels of sugar in the blood.

document: To create a record through writing, film, or photographs.

drought: A long period of time during which there is very little or no rain.

generation: A group of people born and living around the same time.

irrigation: The supplying of water to land by man-made means.

lease: A legal agreement that lets someone use something for a period of time in return for payment.

loom: A tool used for making cloth by weaving yarn or thread.

negotiate: To discuss a way to reach an agreement on a problem.

pasture: A piece of land that animals feed upon.

poet laureate: A poet honored for achievement.

puberty: The period during which a young person becomes capable of reproducing.

raid: A sudden attack.

reservation: Land set aside by the government for specific Native American tribes to live on.

uranium: A silvery metal used to make nuclear energy.

FOR MORE INFORMATION

BOOKS

Benoit, Peter, and Kevin Cunningham. *The Navajo*. New York, NY: Children's Press, 2011.

Denetdale, Jennifer. *The Navajo*. New York, NY: Chelsea House, 2011.

Tieck, Sarah. *Navajo*. Minneapolis, MN: ABDO Publishing, 2015.

WEBSITES

Due to the changing nature of Internet links, PowerKids Press has developed an online list of websites related to the subject of this book. This site is updated regularly. Please use this link to access the list: www.powerkidslinks.com/sona/nav

INDEX